Heaven's Golden Vessel

Heaven's Golden Vessel

Ex-Professional Boxer and Ex-VooDoo Priest Tells Story of Going to Heaven and Hell after a Brain Aneurysm.

Dr. Curtis "Earthquake" Kelley

Copyright (C) 2005 by Curtis Kelley

All Rights Reserved. No part of this publication may be reproduced, stored in a retrieval system or transmitted in any form or by any means - electronic, mechanical, photocopy, recording or any other - except for brief quotations in printed review, without the prior permission of the publisher.

Scripture quotations are taken from The King James Version of the Bible. Public Domain.

Disclaimer: The information provided on aneurysms has been provided for a personal testimony only. This is not medical advice. If you need medical advice, consult with a licensed professional.

Dedication

This book is dedicated to my wife, Selena, who gave me the courage to go on when many times it looked very dark after the aneurysm.

I also dedicate this book to my children, Keme, Zina, Curtis Jr., Angela, Christopher, and Cherish.

I dedicate this to my son, Scott, who now lives in Heaven with Jesus.

This book is also dedicated to my mother, Erma Jean Kelley, and all my brothers and sisters.

I must mention one of my sisters by name, Chandler, because she helped me type the book.

And I cannot forget my wonderful in-laws, Freddie and Barbara Jean Edwards, who always told me to never stop.

Finally, I dedicate this book to all of my children.

But most of all, I dedicate this book to my Lord and Savior, Jesus Christ. He saved my soul from a burning Hell and allowed me to take a look at what is ahead on the other side in Heaven for those who love Him.

Table of Contents

CHAPTERS

Preface

1. The Brain Aneurysm............................9
2. The Hospital Room...................... 24
3. The Warning............................... 32
4. No More Morphine 36
5. The Uninvited Guests................ 45
6. The Offer................................... 51
7. My Friendly Visit........................ 56
8. The Golden Vessel..................... 60
9. The Light................................... 67
10. The Crystal River 75
11. The Testimony 87
12. The Heart of God 94
13. Chosen 104
14. The Reminder 115
15. When I Got Back 119

Preface

There is nothing worse than going through something as bad as what I went through on December 1, 2004. Many people have been through terrible things, but they don't deem it important enough to testify about it. I must tell everyone around the world what the Lord has done for me and tell from where God has brought me. God sent me back from the dead to warn humankind of the dangers of sin, to show everyone how serious it is not to repent of sin, and to show the world how sin hurts God. Before December 1, 2004, I did not know that the Creator of the Universe could hurt in such a way due to the sinful state of human kind. God gave me a mandate and sent me back to Earth. I am more than grateful to God for this assignment, and I gave God my word that I would tell the world what He instructed me to share. The Bible says, "We overcome by the blood of the lamb and by the word of our testimony." (Revelations 12:11) The daily news reports show people turning their backs on God every day.

God instructed me to write book to warn the world about the pain that sin causes Him. When God specifically addresses a subject in the Bible that concerns him, it is to be taken to heart. There is nothing that concerns him more than the sin of disobedience. Sin drives a wedge between us and God. In the past I never thought of myself as a prophet but now I see that God has called me after the brain aneurysm, to be a prophet sent back from the dead to warn this world of dangers of sin and rebellion against the Creator.

As you read this book, if anything you read applies to you, you should run to God so he can cover all your sins with the blood of the final sacrificial lamb, Jesus Christ. The Bible says, "Believe his prophets so shall you prosper." (II Chronicle 20:20) Invite a friend to also read this book. Tell them that the book has eternal value.

Chapter 1
The Brain Aneurysm

The date was December 1, 2004. After coming home from a Wednesday night Bible study, I was sitting on the edge of my bed about to go to sleep. Something was happening to my head. It felt like hot water was being poured on top of my head. I looked around to see if someone was there; however, no one was in the room. My wife and children were nowhere to be found. As I was trying to figure out what was going on, a very powerful type of electrical shock hit me in the center of my head. It felt like a hundred volts hit me. I could feel it all the way down to my shoulders.

Next, the pain that hit me was like twenty men punching me with their fists or whatever they could get in their hands. I had never had pain like this in my life. This pain was one hundred times worse than any headache that I ever had. I know that this headache was from hell. I could feel the presence of demonic activity all around me. It seemed like the demons were laughing at me because I think they thought they had me for sure this time. They thought this night was my last night on Earth. It was like assassins were sent to bump me off. I knew I was in trouble.

Usually I do not call my wife, Selena, on her cell phone over a headache but this was not something that I wanted to keep to myself. The spirit of death and his gang were in my room telling me that it was my time to die. I had no idea that I was having an aneurysm. I did not know that I was actually dying. I did not know that fifteen percent of all people having an aneurysm die before the reach the hospital according to the doctors at hospital. At that point, having that knowledge would not have helped me.

Heaven's Golden Vessel

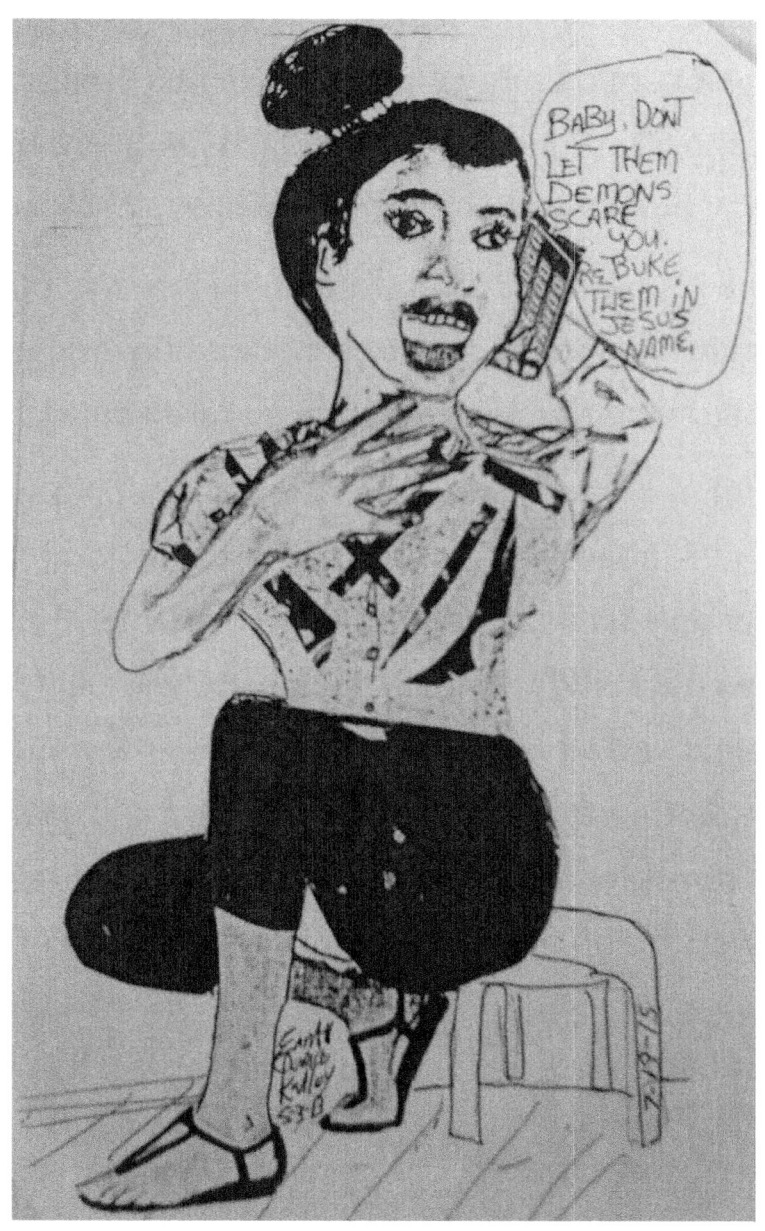

I have become an expert on aneurysms after going through this experience. I learned that sentinel headaches are warnings of something deadly to come. Most of us pay no attention to this type of headache. This kind of headache is telling you that you may only have two hours to two weeks to live.

I also learned that more than twenty-five percent of people experience seizures close to the onset of the aneurysm. Nausea and vomiting are some of the symptoms as well. I was sick to my stomach prior to having the aneurysm. I could not keep my food down. Most people have symptoms of meningeal irritation such as neck stiffness, low back pain, and bilateral leg pain. I had all of this, but I did not know what it meant. During this time I started going blind as well. I never wore glasses but during the aneurysm, my eyes were so bleary that I could hardly see anything. I developed a type of photophobia which means that sunlight hurt my eyes and the top of my head.

Before an aneurysm hits, you have a loss of consciousness due to bleeding in your brain. The bible says, "My people are destroyed for the lack of knowledge." (Hosea 4:6) My lack of knowledge almost cost me my life.

As I sat there on the side of my bed, I felt my blood pulsating hard through the veins in my head. It was so extreme that I had to put my fingers on each side of head to block the flow of blood.

Heaven's Golden Vessel

It was a good thing that the blood did not leak from my ears because my bedroom floor would have been flooded with blood. The more it pumped up my neck and into my head the worse the pain became that night. I felt as though I was passing out. I had to fight to stay awake. I thought if I passed out, I would die from possibly falling and landing in a way that I could not breathe and ultimately suffocate given my large size.

My sister, Chandler, was down the hall in the next room, and I called out to her, but she did not hear me. It was hard to talk and even harder to yell, because the aneurysm caused my throat to shrink to the size of a drinking straw. My children had turned in for the night because it was a school night, and they had to be up very early the next morning. When the unbearable pain started happening to me, they were fast asleep.

The blood started to boil in my skull like an oven being heated to approximately four hundred degrees. I then thought, "Lord, what is going on here?" It felt as though the forces of Hell were all unleashed and trying to destroy me. My eyesight was getting dim as though I was looking out through a fog, and my hearing was getting dull as I lost consciousness. I did not know what was going on with me, but God knew. God let me regain consciousness. It felt like hands were trying to put me on the floor. I was fighting with all of my might to stay on the bed. The back of my head was on fire and it felt like my head was hot enough to burn my fingers. I was very scared. I knew if I fell to the floor, I would not get up. The spirit of fear was trying to control me.

Heaven's Golden Vessel

My wife, Selena, had not come home from church yet and I begin to reminiscing about how she had been by my side through many tests and sickness. In 1990, the doctors found cancer in my neck and it was the size of a baseball. The doctors told me that there was no chance that I would live past six months. Selena told me to disregard what those doctors said because God was going to heal me, and He did. That night it seemed like she was a million light years away but she was on the other end of her cell phone telling me to hold on. I thank her for being the wife and mother that she is, and I love her.

As I thought about that strange pain inside my head that night, I also wondered what would happen to my family if I were to die that night but one the other end of the phone, Selena was still there telling me that she would take me to the emergency room when she arrived home. She would not hang up on me until she walked through our front door. When Selena arrived home, she told me to get ready to go to the hospital. I told her I would be fine, to just let me sleep on it, and that if it did not go away tomorrow I would go to the hospital.

The next day, it got worse. My wife was still trying to get me to go the hospital. I finally changed my mind completely regarding going to the hospital as the pain became even worse. It was a man thing. That man thing almost killed me. My wife stayed on me until she finally got me to go to the hospital.

As I thought about my past profession as a boxer, I thought perhaps I had one too many punches, and it had finally caught up with me. I had forty fights and lost only three fights. Days later, I found out from my doctor that my condition had nothing to do with boxing. I then wondered what was really wrong with me.

As I started getting ready to go to the hospital, I bent over to put on my shoes and as my blood raced to my head it felt like explosions going on in my skull. I had to sit down on the couch due to the sharp pains and dizziness. I knew that I was in trouble. As I walked to the car my wife offered to help me and told her could make it. At that time, I could barely see the car right in front of me. I was trying to be strong. It was that man thing telling me, I shouldn't show it. Pride can kill you.

Chapter 2
The Hospital Room

On my way to the hospital, the night air felt good to my head. It was a very cool evening. Because I could not really see the car, I put my arms out in front of me as far as I could so if I stumbled, I would collapse on the car to break my fall. Every step I took was like I was walking with a blindfold on my eyes. Finally, I put my hands on top of the car which was ice cold. I then put my hands made cold by the car on my head to try to numb the pain and cool the heater going off in the back of my head, but it did not work. I do not remember taking the ride to the hospital because I was in a deep sleep upon arrival. I could not open my eyes and I remember asking my wife, "Where are we?" She told me we were at the hospital.

I was just interested in getting out of the pain I was in at that moment. I remember refusing the wheelchair when we arrived at the hospital. It was that man thing kicking in again and in my sick state I still managed to stumble into the emergency room.

I should have sat in the wheel chair because it was difficult for me to stand up. When we found an empty seat, I sat down so hard that I felt as though I broke bones in my lower back. As my wife tried to answer questions for me, the nurse informed her that I had to answer the questions myself. I could not even pronounce my own name at the time. I was literally outside of my mind because the pain was so intense. When the lady behind the counter asked my name, I barely responded.

She asked me again, "What is your name?' I said, "Kelley." The nurse asked, "Is Kelley the first or last name?" I told her yes and that I was very sick and could not answer any more questions. She saw that I was in very bad shape, and she said, "Take a seat Mr. Kelley. I'll talk to your wife." My wife gave her all of the information that she needed. Finally, they put me in a room. I started coming back to myself after two hours. By then, I was laughing with my wife and the nurses on duty. However, I did not really know how sick I was, and no one would tell me. I'm not sure they really knew at that time.

The nurses on duty were doing all they could to stop the pain, but nothing was working. One of the doctors said, "Let's give him some morphine. We have tried everything else within reason and nothing seems to help."

They put a needle in my left arm and attempted fifteen times to find my vein. My veins always have been hard to find. They were probing under my skin for what seemed like an hour. I said, "Please put me asleep and do it." They all laughed but it was not funny.

When they found the right place in my arm, the blood started flowing. At that point, I just wanted to thank Jesus for dying on the cross because of his blood that flowed for me. I could just imagine what it must have been like to have someone put long nails through your hands. Jesus really suffered greatly for us all. God is so good. Even at my sickest point, I could still feel God's healing virtue in that moment.

Another doctor mentioned that I may have had an aneurysm and to be sure they had to do a spinal tap. Another doctor said he could get the fluid out of my spine. I instantly thought, "No! If you can't find my veins in my arms, how are you going to find fluid inside of my spine"?

I thought, "You must be crazy if you think that you are going to stick those three inch needles in my back" My wife said, "Sweetie, you have to let them do it." I said, "No way Dear. If they can't find the veins in my arm, I'm not going to let them probe inside of my back. Suppose they hit the wrong thing. I might be paralyzed forever."

My wife said to let them do it because it was the only way to find out what was really wrong with me. She told me, "You could die if you don't let them do it, Sweetie."

I gave in and agreed with her. The doctor said, "I will take you down to the lab and put you on our special x-ray machine. We always find the fluid with it." They took me downstairs and hooked me up to that machine and sure enough they were pulling fluid out of my back like it was coming out of a spring. It wasn't like what they did to me upstairs. Up there, it felt like a jackhammer was being administered. It was painful.

One hour after they pulled the pencil long needle from my back, they came back with the report saying, "Just like we thought, it's a subarachnoid hemorrhage, an aneurysm of the brain". The doctor further stated, "if you had waited one more day, you would have died at home. Some folk die within an hour of having burst blood vessels or an aneurysm".

Chapter 3
The Warnings

I still did not get it. How could something like this happen to me? I praise God for Jesus. He was the only one who made it possible for me to escape death. Many of us get warnings but we don't know what to think of the warnings in our lives.

There were warning signs with my aneurysm. The headaches were warnings called prodromal warnings. This happens for us in the natural realm as well as in the spiritual realm. Many people in the Bible understood prodromal warnings. Noah gave the world a warning. The prodromal warning alerts us that something bad is coming and signals us to take an action of repentance.

The Word of God gives us a lot of prodromal warnings. I had been given many warnings about my health. I should have gone to my personal doctor to have those very bad headaches checked out. I almost didn't go, and it almost killed me. If we take care of ourselves, our heads should never hurt. The wrong diet, worry and don't forget stress can give us terrible headaches.

I remember being in fellowship with a church that gave me so much stress. I was walking around that place like I was walking on egg shells. There was a strong spirit of Jezebel controlling it. God told me to leave, but the spirit of Jezebel would not let me go. I would be okay while driving to church, but once my family and I arrived at the parking lot of the church, it felt like pressure from Hell. My head would only hurt while I was there, and once I was off the property, I was just fine.

God hates the spirit of Jezebel. Why? Because it pushes the spirit of God out of His Church. Whoever would have thought that a church could cause so much pain? Many of you reading this book are at a church that is being controlled by the spirit of Jezebel. Don't let these churches be the cause of your life ending prematurely.

Heaven's Golden Vessel

I was taking my time at home not really understanding that what was going on in my head that night was a result of a life stress and poor eating habits. I thank God for a wife that would not let me just sit at home and die. She is the one who would not let me be stubborn. I thought that it was just another bad headache.

The hospital staff brought me back upstairs but my head still hurt like hell was attacking. When all the other medicine failed, the doctors went back to giving me morphine. I thought, "Hey, we are not in any war zone. Why are you giving me that stuff? I am not shot. I do not have any bullet wounds". However, having an aneurysm is like being shot in the head and having the blood pour out.

With an aneurysm, the blood vessels explode on the inside of your head, and death comes within the hour in most cases. The doctors were astonished and wondered what kept me alive. The answer is Jesus!

Chapter 4
No Morphine Please

Before they gave me the morphine, I was dealing with the headache and the pain through laughter. As the morphine worked its way through my veins it felt like lava was running through my veins. The lava felt like acid burning inside coupled with a ton of pressure.

Then it felt like those demonic presences at my house were now standing on my chest, and they were cutting off my air. It felt like their feet and their pointy toenails were on my stomach. It also felt like an elephant's foot was on my chest. After that, I felt as though I was falling from a tall building. Then fear and his buddy torment entered the room.

I tried to grab a hold of the sides of the hospital bed. Then I started to shake like a leaf in a storm. I was able to hear everything the doctors were doing to save my life and I was able to feel the presence of at least ten doctors and nurses working on me. I was shaking very violently and the side of the room appeared to be turning upside down. I thought, "God, don't let them choke me to death in front of my wife! Please Lord Jesus, don't let me die in front of my wife"? I was having convulsion due to them giving me morphine. By the grace of God, I survived. A short time later, the doctors told me they thought that they lost me. Nobody including myself knew that I was allergic to morphine. Today, I believe the enemy was trying to kill me.

That same night the devil tried to kill me again. A nurse came back and tried to pump me with morphine. I could not defend myself physically or verbally but God always has a ram in the bush. A nurse who was there when they initially gave me the morphine saw what I went through earlier and she stood up for me and said "No, you can't give him anymore. It almost killed him earlier." When this helpful nurse was not around, other doctors prescribed the morphine in pill form for me and a male nurse told me to be careful of what they are giving me. I thanked him for warning me. I witnessed to him about being saved and he said, "Yes I am and praise God. The devil lost another one."

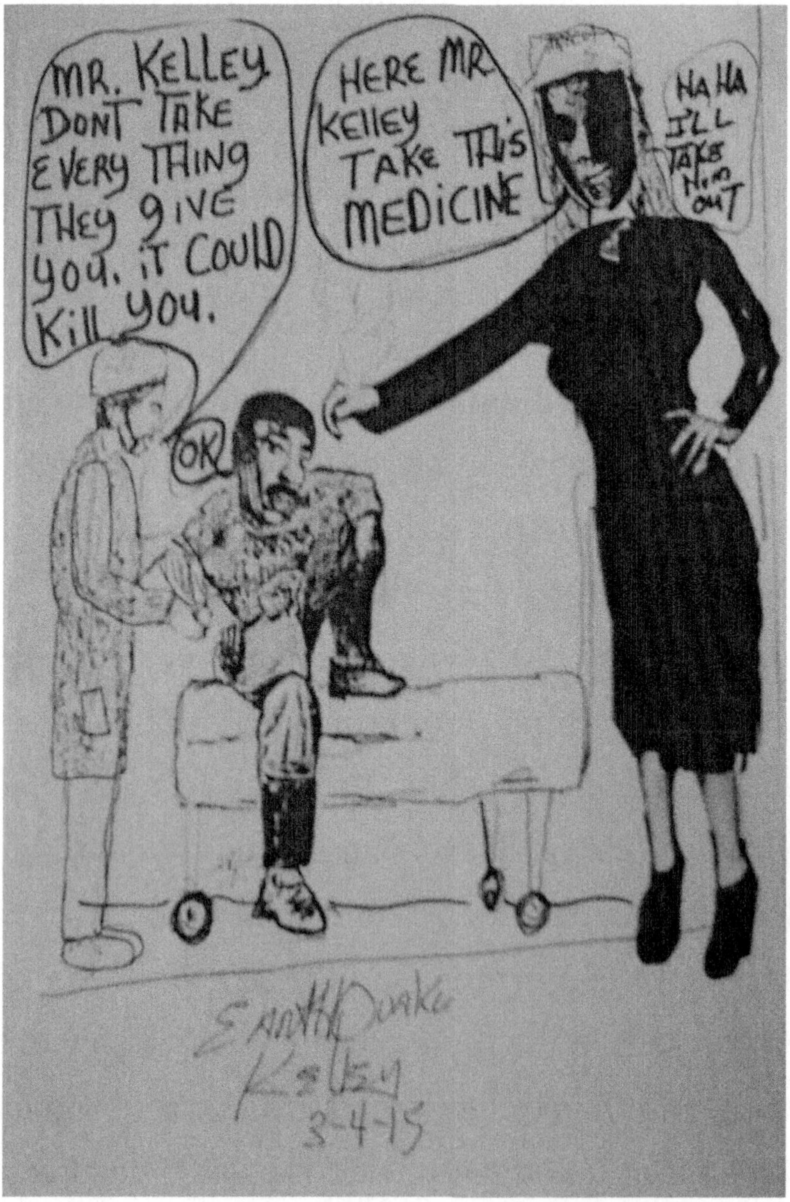
MR. KELLEY DONT TAKE EVERY THING THEY GIVE YOU. IT COULD KILL YOU.
HERE MR. KELLEY TAKE THIS MEDICINE
HA HA I'LL TAKE HIM OUT
OK

He then said, "Don't take the medicine and ask questions. They could be giving you something that could act like poison in your body." He kept telling me to be careful. I believe God placed him on duty just to help me, because I could not help myself.

Shortly thereafter, a nurse came in with a pill and water. When I questioned her, she told me that it was morphine in pill form as the doctor ordered. I asked her for permission to call my wife and ask her first. When I called my wife and asked her if I should take the morphine, my wife became angry and said, "No, do not take it." I told the nurse that my wife said not to take it. The enemy was trying everything to destroy my life that night but he failed again. The Lord healed me twice from cancer and once with heart trouble.

WHAT ARE you DOING? MORPHINE WILL KILL MR. KELLEY THEY GAVE IT TO HIM LAST NIGHT, HE ALMOST DIED!
MY HUSBAND Allergic TO MORPHINE

Satan has tried deadly things to take me out fifty other times. Now he tried to take me out with morphine but it failed. Praise Jesus!

I remember being at a baseball game when a guy tried to cut my throat. An invisible hand pulled me out of the way. He cut my left cheek and missed my throat. I could have bled to death if I had been cut. The switchblade left a big scar on my face. The enemy thought he could take me out but praise God the Lord said, "Not So".

Now lying in the hospital bed, my head was hurting so bad that they had to put two blocks of ice on my temples. I had six blocks of ice on my head and three on each side, and the ice melted very quickly because of the heat generated by the pain of the headache.

My family was very faithful with coming to see me, but my children endured great pain seeing me suffer. My son, Chris, walked out of the hospital room. He could not stand to see me in that kind of shape. He is a great son. I love my sons so much. I have two living sons, Curtis, Jr. and Chris. Their older brother, Scott, was killed, and it was so hard for my two sons to go through that. Now it looked like they were going to lose their dad too. It was too much for Chris to see me like that. He walked out crying one day after the nurses tried to feed me my dinner. It was an event. Aneurysms shrink your throat down to the size of a drinking straw. The smallest thing can choke you. A piece of food got stuck, and I started choking. My son, Chris, saw me coughing and fighting for air. He couldn't take it. I felt sorrier for him than I did for myself.

There was a nurse on duty that said she was a Christian but she would always tell me that she did not do death too good. She said that she was afraid of dead bodies. One day, she asked me, "You ain't going to die on me, are you Mr. Kelley? I do not do dead bodies so don't die while I am in here with you". Another day she came to the door of the hospital room to check on me. She knocked on the door of my room and asked, "Mr. Kelley, are you alive"? She kept knocking at the door and got louder and louder, as if I could respond because of the condition of my throat.

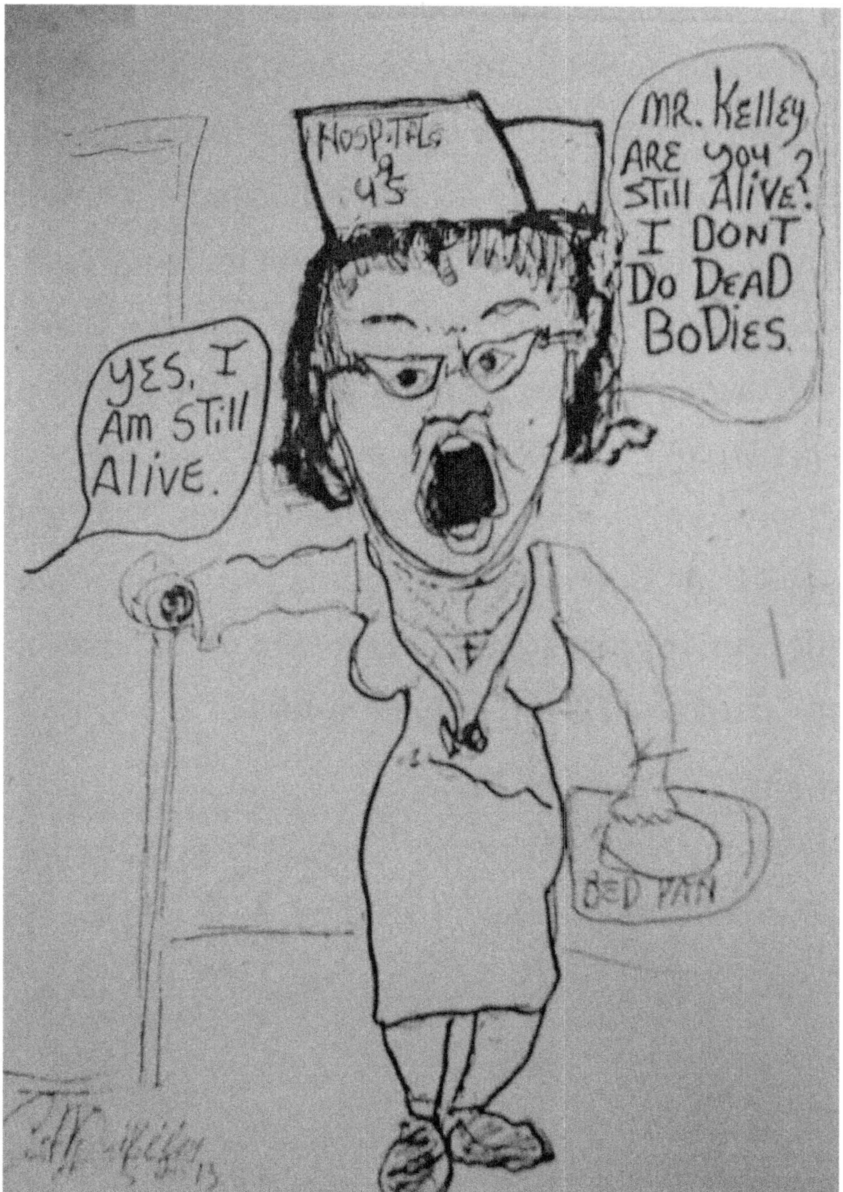
MR. Kelley ARE you STill Alive? I DONT Do DEAD BoDies.
YES, I Am STill Alive.
BED PAN

Then I saw her doing something that will never forget in all the days of my life. She poked her head in the door and yelled, "Mr. Kelley, are you still alive"? I got some power from somewhere and yelled back, "Yes, I am alive". She said, "Good because I was about to call the guy from the morgue to come pick up your body". I told her, "Not yet because I am still using it". I thought, "What kind of mess is that? I am still alive." It was a shame that this Christian woman was afraid of dead people and works where people die every day. Well, it happens I guess. The Bible says that "God has not given us the spirit of fear but the spirit of power and of love and of a sound mind." (II Timothy 1:7) I am praying for her.

Chapter Five
The Uninvited Guests

    The doctors and nurses had to watch me twenty four hours a day. They were coming and going like it was Grand Central Station. I was blessed to have people come from Los Angeles and some from out of town to see me and pray for me. One day, it was about ten in the morning and the nurses were coming and going. I was so glad to be alive and see the sun shining in the window. I turned on the television just to hear some news or whatever was on television like a game show. I don't like violent programming. I grew up with violence in my community, so I don't need to see it on television.

    As I was channel surfing, two men came into my room, walking right by the nurse and she never acknowledges them. I thought that this was strange because usually if someone walks by someone would say good morning, especially in a public place. As they came in, one man sat down in a chair near the foot of my bed and the other man just stood there looking at me. The one that sat down started mumbling and saying things under his breath. He was saying words that people who practice witchcraft use on people to place curse on them. He also had a look of disgust on his face and I knew these men were not Christians. They actually came to do me harm.

Then I noticed that neither one of these men had on shirts. I thought to myself, why weren't they stopped by the nurses' station without being properly dressed"? One of these men had an extra- large head which looked like he had a tumor in it. I said to myself, "Wow! That guy has a large head. Maybe he should get that thing lanced while he is here." It was funny to me, because I needed a laugh at that time.

WE, BEEN TRYING TO KILL YOU, FOR YEARS
WHY, WONT YOU DIE?
SEE MY LONG, MIDDLE FINGER IN YOUR FACE?
NO, YOU DIDNT, JUST CURSE AT ME! I'M GETTING OUT OF THIS I BET
THE BLOOD OF JESUS
I REBUKE YOU IN THE NAME OF JESUS

The one sitting on the chair looked at me and said, "We have been trying to kill you for a long time, but somehow you always manage to escape." I could not talk above a whisper and I said, "What did you say?" I then knew they were no friends of mine. I heard the voice of the Lord say, "These are not human beings. They are from the kingdom of Hell. Their master, the Devil, sent them. Do not try to fight them with your fists. It won't do you any good, son. Use the name of Jesus." Being a fighter, I wanted to get out of that bed and fight them with my fist. But in the natural I was very weak. I was hardly able to make a fist.

The Lord quoted the Bible and said that "the weapons of our warfare are not carnal but mighty through God to the pulling down of strongholds."(II Corinthians 10:4) The same passage tells us to "cast down imaginations, and every high thing that exalts itself against the knowledge of God, and bring into captivity every thought to the obedience of Christ". (II Corinthians 10:5) Even though I couldn't jump out of that bed and try to fight those evil spirits with my hands, I would have been in disobedience if I had tried to fight because God told me not to fight in my own strength but to use the power that he placed inside of me through Jesus Christ.

For years, the enemy has been trying to kill me. These demonic spirits were around for some time that day yelling, poking fun in my ear, and one even put up his middle finger at me. I finally said, "In the name of Jesus, leave this room!" As soon as they heard the name of Jesus, they disappeared. I immediately phoned my wife and told her what had happened. She ministered to me saying, "Continue calling on the name of Jesus. Baby don't let them scare you". I realized I was actually in the midst of a spiritual battle for my life. The demonic activity came in and like a flood God came through for me with the standard of His mighty Word. (Isaiah 59:19)

On December 4, 2004, as I was lying on my bed in the intensive care unit suffering from the effects of a brain aneurysm, I said, "Oh my God, I am in so much pain.' I was greatly afraid and as soon as I called on the name of Jesus, his presence came in my room and left peace in my spirit. If you keep your mind on the Lord, he will keep you in perfect peace.

(Isaiah 26:3+4)

The nurses and doctors entered in what seemed to be every fifteen minutes to poke, probe, and/or adjust my oxygen tube. They said, "You would be dead in minutes if we did not check on you minute by minute because this condition is not one to be played with." One of the doctors paced back and forth by my room looking in at me every day. When they came in they asked "Are you sure you are okay? Do you have any paralysis?' I would always respond, "I am okay", and move my hands and feet to show them I was still with them. Except for those headaches, I felt fine. The look on the doctor's face let me know that something was very wrong with me, I was a dead man. As far as the doctors were concerned, they were waiting for me to stop breathing and they believed this was just hours away.

Chapter 6
The Offer

One doctor in particular who reminded me of Groucho Marx in appearance, asked me every day, "Are you okay"? He had so much concern for my condition. So I asked him one day, "Doc, am I going to die? You seem to be extremely worried about me". He answered a question with a question which was, "How is it that you are still alive? You are in very bad shape Mr. Kelley! Most people die within two hours with this kind of sickness".

He then asked me again, "How is it that you are still alive"? Then he said, Mr. Kelley, how would you like to go to India with me? I want the people of India to see you. You are a miracle. All over the world very, very few people live past two days. I have to take you to my country." I said, "Yes I'll go to India to show off for you." I think he wants to get some of the credit for my healing. But I'll preach while he is doing his medical show.

MR. Kelley you Dont HAVE ANY PARALYSIS?
MOVE YOUR HANDS. MOVE YOUR FEET!
I'M, GOING TO TAKE YOU TO INDIA, TO SHOW ALL MY FRIENDS THE ONLY MAN THAT SURVIVED AN A N OF THE BRAIN
WHAT. is Keeping you ALIVE?
JESUS
SURE, I LOVE TO GO TO INDIA

The trip is scheduled for January 2006. Souls will be saved in India. So far, God has taken me to Pakistan, China, London, Ireland, Haiti, Mexico and a free trip to India would be a blessing. I believe all things work together for the good including this brain aneurysm. (Romans 8:28)

The nurses gave me continuous amounts of pills to help reduce the damage caused by bleeding in the brain from the burst blood vessel. These pills were almost the size of my pinkie. And if you have seen the size of my hands, you know that those pills were large. Only by the grace of God I was able to swallow them. Plus I had very high blood pressure. It was two hundred over two hundred at times. They had the hardest time trying to get my blood pressure back down.

My head hurt so badly during my stay in the hospital. Most people do not know what it is like to have a headache until you have had a brain aneurysm headache. It is like your head is being beat in by twenty men using lead pipe in the temples with all their might.

One day the doctor saw that I was in great pain and asked me if I wanted to have my head packed in ice. I said, Yes, please put my head in some ice, please"! They brought me two blocks of ice. Oh my God, it felt so wonderful. My head was so hot that it would melt those blocks of ice like they were placed on the top of an oven. It was like this every day. That's why they had to check my very high blood pressure every fifteen minutes. They had me on death watch around the clock. However, one day at the usual time, no one came in to check on me. I thought to myself "Now I can get that much needed break I have been longing for." I turned off the television and just began to praise God in spite of the tubes in my left arm and the uncomfortable tube stuck in my right hand.

One day as my wife was visiting me, I just wanted her to take the tube out of my hand and nose because I felt like a prisoner strapped down. I lifted my hands as best I could and began praying in the spirit and the praises started ringing. I tried to turn on my right side. However, the oxygen cord was too short and so I just laid on my back and prayed.

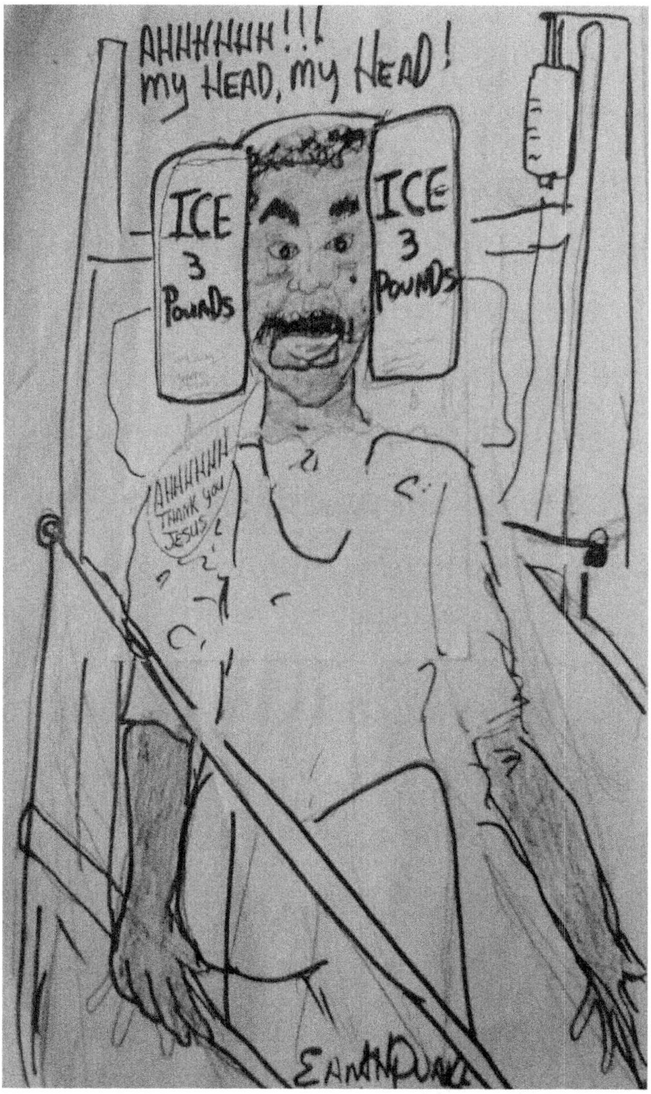
AHHHHHH!!!
my HEAD, my HEAD!
ICE 3 POUNDS
ICE 3 POUNDS
AHHHHHH THANK you JESUS

Chapter 7
My Friendly Visit

I was lying in the hospital bed looking up at the ceiling reflecting on all the things that I had been through over the last few days and how close I came to dying again. Why did I find myself here in the hospital? God, I am sick and in so much pain. I did not know what was wrong with me and no one would tell me. The people that came to see me would not tell me. I heard them talking about an aneurysm, but I think that they didn't want to scare me. They thought telling me would have made me worse than I already was.

One day, a very good pastor friend came to see me. He drove over two hundred miles to see me. It just so happen that at the same time he came to see me, it was time for a CAT scan. I did not care too much for it because I did not like going in that long tunnel. I had to be very careful because the blood in my head would move around like it was trying to find a place to come out.

When I saw him walk in my room, I was so glad to see him. He surprised me. I said, "Man, did you drive all the way to see me"? He said, "Earthquake, I would drive across the country to see about you". I wanted to cry but it took too much energy to get my tear ducts to work. Crying would cause the headaches from hell to get worse.

Well, the staff began to put me in the wheel chair so we can head toward to the next building, which was a block away. It was cold up in the mountains where the hospital is located, my body became ice cold. But my head loved that icy night air. It was so refreshing.

My pastor friend walked the entire way with me to the CAT scan building. I could see the tears forming in his eyes as they put me on the table. I was so weak that I could hardly move from the wheel chair to the table by myself. He said, "Earthquake, I can't stand to watch them put you in there." The technician working the machine told him that he could stay. He said, "Earthquake, I can't stay." I felt bad for my friend, because he felt so bad for me. Before he left, he prayed for me and gave me some scriptures.

Heaven's Golden Vessel

The one I remember is "God is our refuge and strength, a very present help in trouble. (Psalm 46:1) He then left. The staff took me back to my room and put me back to bed. I felt lonely back at the hospital room. I really wanted to go home. The enemy was trying to make me hold grudges against people who did not come to see me, like the pastor I was submitted to at the time. I was faithful to that ministry and nobody did not come or call. The devil wanted me to think on this in my fragile state to try to make my situation worse. This is a strategy from hell to cause a stroke or heart attack. I had to forgive them and forgive them I did. The moment I got that off my mind, I felt the Lord's this is what permitted the healing to continue.

Chapter 8
The Golden Vessel

One night as I was resting in the hospital bed, I started praising God for sparing my life again. I turned off the television so I could put my mind entirely on God. As I was meditating on God, the nurse came into the room to check on me. I told her that I was in pain but other than that I was okay. On her way out of the room, she asked, "Do you want me to close the door?" I said, "Yes, please close the door. Thank you." I wanted the door closed, because I wanted to have church in my room by myself. I wanted to be free to lift my hands up as far as I could get them and speak freely in my prayer language.

I praised and thanked God so much that night to the point that I became breathless. After my praise break, I rested my head completely on the pillow and tears began to come down my face. Even though it was difficult to cry, it felt so good to cry in the presence of the Lord.

As I rested and cried, I noticed the room was not completely dark because of the street lights. The room began to get brighter and brighter and I stopped crying becoming acute aware of the increasing amount of light in the room. As I looked to find the source of the light in my room, I saw something coming down from the ceiling. It was not like anything I had ever seen before. I could not take my eyes off it. I was totally blown away with it and in awe as I felt the presence of God filling the whole room as this beautiful golden thing descended through the ceiling of my hospital room and settled at the foot of my bed. It was a golden vessel. I could not see the entire vessel due to the fact that I was not able to get out of the bed on my own. But it was so beautiful. It appeared to have flakes of pure gold. As I looked in amazement, it became clear to me that someone who was a great artist designed this wonderful thing.

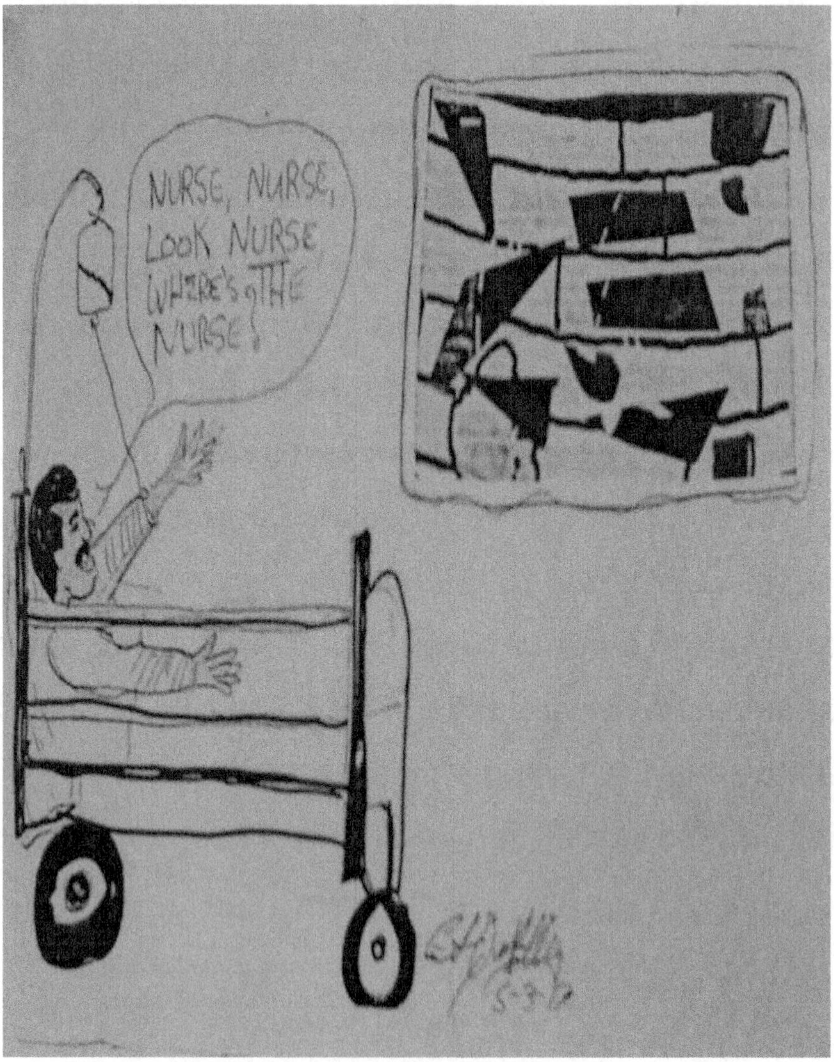
NURSE, NURSE, LOOK NURSE WHERE'S THE NURSE!

But as I was lying there looking at this thing, I wondered why something of such wonder came to me? Who am I? The only well know thing I ever did was try to box, and I am only a little known at that. During the early years of my life I was a thug. Then it came to me. It has nothing to do with what you were growing up. It is what God saw in me. As I was praising God, I said, "God you must really think a whole lot of me to send this vessel into my sick room." Then I knew that I was going to die for sure because things like this only come to take someone away. I thank God it was not a freight train from hell coming to get me. I did not know if I should try to touch it or not. The golden brilliance I thought would make a real nice piece of jewelry. It is great to maintain a sense of humor in the moments of life and death.

I wondered where all of the doctors and nurses were at the moment. They should see the vessel. It was time for my blood pressure check and time for the medicine but not one of them came in the room to check on me. As I look back, I think God did not want them to see it. It was just for me.

Heaven's Golden Vessel

The golden vessel lifted me out of that hospital bed, I felt light as a feather. I began to hover over my body and I remember looking over my body thinking that guy lying there is in very bad shape. As I looked at that man lying there, it dawned on me that the man lying there in the hospital bed almost dead was me. But how? How can I be up here looking down at my body? Is that my empty shell? I could see my lifeless body with the tubes in my arm and the oxygen cord up my nose. I had no idea that I was so bad off. I thought, "Earthquake Kelley, you are gone. When the nurses come, they will find me dead." But I did not feel any sorrow. Then I wondered what was going to happen next? Will I just hang around the ceiling or come down?

Many people die terrible deaths. I gently passed away. That golden vessel was so gentle. It carried me to a place where it was so peaceful. That beautiful golden vessel enveloped me like a blanket and gently took me away to paradise. The Bible is true. It says, "To be absent from the body is to be present with the Lord." (II Corinthians 5:8) As I departed from my body, I praised God for being saved. The Word of God

lets us know that precious in the sight of the Lord is the death of His saints. (Psalm 116:15) If you are not saved and do not know the Lord in the pardoning of your sins, you will not see the Lord's face in peace. I admonish you in this hour to repent, ask the Lord Jesus into your life, and commit your life to Him. He will give you the strength to live according to His will while you are here on Earth, and you will have eternal life too.

Chapter 9
The Light

Now back to the hospital room, where I was hovering over my body. In a blink of an eye the golden vessel carried me to a place so beautiful that I will try my best to explain. There were angels waiting for me and they were covered from their head to their toes with some type of gold stuff. They were so bright that it was hard to look upon them. The light was not coming directly from them it came from over and around them and it was so powerful. The light coming over them was much more powerful.

I was so happy to be there. The angels opened the door of that golden vessel. I looked at them in amazement as I walked out of the vessel. But as I came out of the vessel, the striking green grass caught my attention immediately. Each blade had a purplish green jewel growing inside of it. It looked like someone had manicured each blade individually taking their time to see to it that each blade was perfect. Each blade of grass looked like it was pointy and sharp.

THE TREES AND ANGELS
Angle look at those trees
So much more to see.
Earthquake Kelley 5-6-13

But as I walked on the grass, it did not hurt my feet as I thought it would because on its appearance. It actually felt like I was walking on cotton. I could have just laid down in it and took hands full of that grass and made me a pillow. The trees were something that you will have to see for yourself.

I saw flowers so large and so lovely that I really cannot describe them. My description would not come close to their beauty. Some flowers were even the size of laundry baskets. I was so excited to see Heaven in all its glory. I knew I had to move on because I did not want to miss a thing in case the golden vessel was coming back to get me. I really felt that I was not going to stay there.

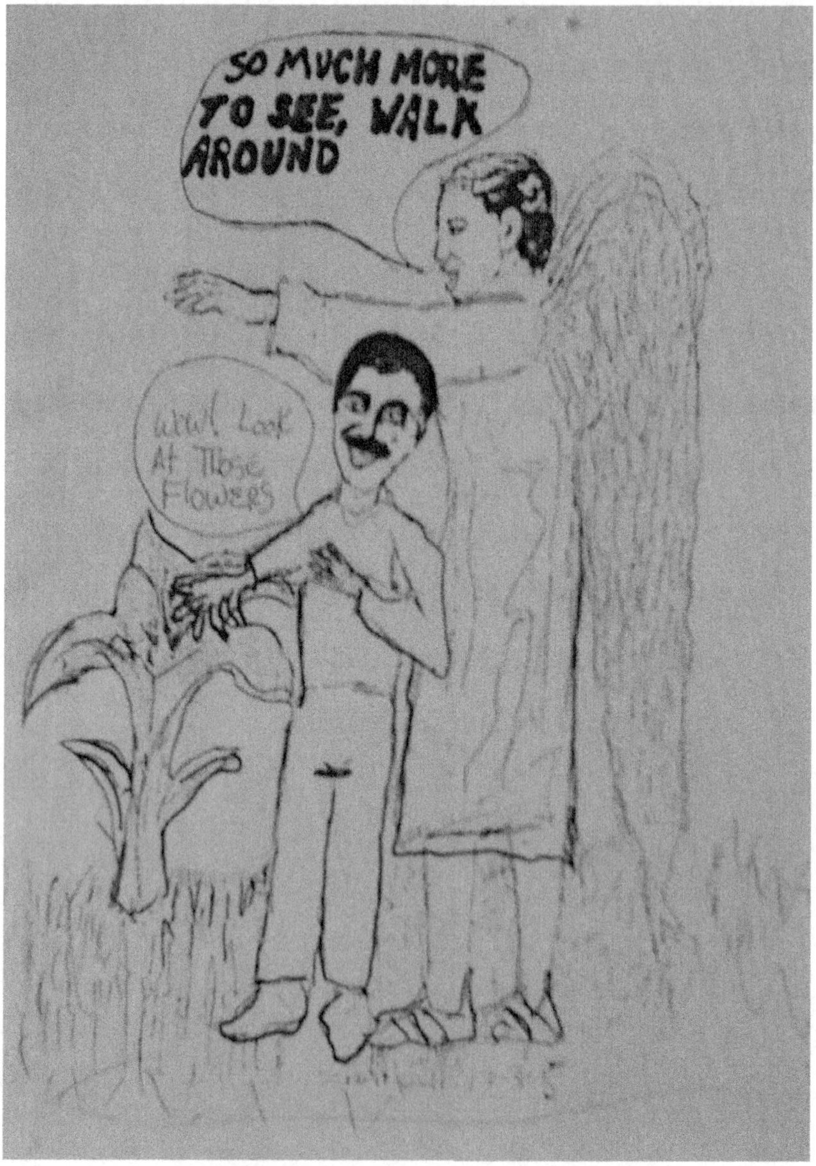
SO MUCH MORE TO SEE, WALK AROUND
WOW! LOOK AT THOSE FLOWERS

I was so excited and blown away at the same time. I thought about running around and leaping into the sky yelling, "Thank you Jesus!" at the top of my voice.

It had not dawned on me what I could or could not do with my body but I knew I was no longer sick. As I examined myself, I no longer had any pain and my vision was improved. Even in the dramatic changes in my body, I was trying to walk far away from the golden vessel as I could to make sure it does not take me back to that hospital room.

I was so appreciative for the vessel that God used to bring me across to the other side. But I said to myself that I no longer have need of the transportation services of the golden vessel. I really did not want to go back to that hospital bed of pain. There was no fear in Heaven like the fear I felt in the hospital room. There was a nurse that had me so afraid. One day she removed my oxygen. I started to choke due to the lack of air. She then walked out of the room. I started to fall out of the bed and onto the floor as I reached for the emergency button. By the grace of God, I was able to reach it. It took all the strength I had. When she finally came back to the room, she just stood there for what seemed like a whole day watching me struggle to breathe. Then when she saw that I was almost dead, she pushed me into the bed like a linebacker making a tackle. My ribs hurt for hours after that moment. I could feel a demonic presence come in the room as she entered every day.

YOU BETTER NOT FALL OUT OF THIS BED AGAIN! IF YOU DO YOU WILL PAY! YOU HEAR ME?
SOMEBODY PLEASE HELP ME!
SHE'S TRYING TO KILL ME.

Here I was in paradise, I could feel the presence of Jesus and not that wicked nurse. The memory of here did not exist there. The presence of my Lord and Savior, Jesus, was there even though I did not see Him. I was extremely joyful. (Psalm 16:11).

While I was in heaven, I started to thank God for the aneurysm because it got me off this evil planet and I was now with my Savior forever. Just imagine the best revival meeting you have ever been in and then magnify it by one thousand times and you can just about feel the atmosphere of the presence of the holy God that we serve. It was like the feeling of God's Spirit was not only in me, but it was also all around me. If I had started dancing, I would have been able to dance and never get tired of dancing before the Lord. They say that a boxer's legs are the first to go. If my Lord saw fit to have kept me there, I would still be dancing. There is so much peace there. I am like Apostle Paul. I can hardly wait to go back. I was so afraid in that hospital room, but I was so full of joy up there. I could just burst. I am getting excited just sharing with you about what happened to me.

Chapter 10
The Crystal River

As I was walking in Heaven, I started to hear music like I had never heard before. I looked to see where it was coming from, and I saw a river. The river was so beautiful. The water looked like liquid diamonds. It was like no other river in the earthly realm. The colors in the water looked like very expensive stained glass. The waves of the water danced as if they were dancing to the music that I was hearing. I was so excited at looking at the river that I ran up to the edge of the bank of the river, and I wanted to stick my feet in the water. I also wanted to cup my hands together and drink from it. I did not know whether I should jump in or just stand there at the bank of that river and sing along with the music I was hearing.

Heaven's Golden Vessel

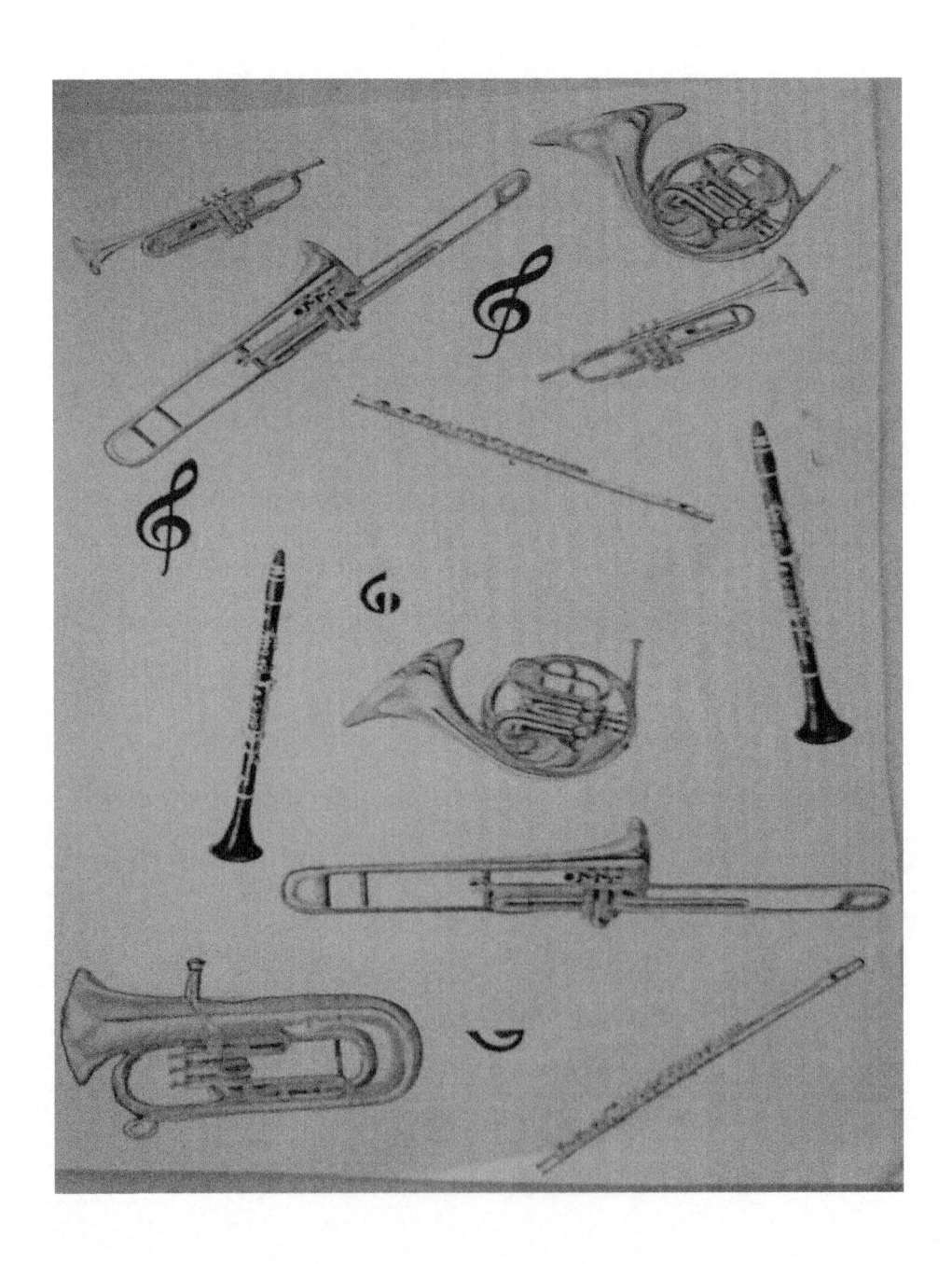

Today, I cannot remember what the words of the music playing were but the melody is stuck in my head. I do not know if I will ever be able to sing it until I get back to Heaven. It was nothing like the songs we sing here on Earth, it was more angelic. I remember saying to myself that only God can write songs like that and build or make a place like this.

Then I thought, "Where are all the saints that passed on and were saved"? If you have lost a loved one who loved Jesus, don't worry about them. Just like my son Scott, they are in Heaven.

As I was standing there along the side of the crystal river, I started thanking God for taking me out of all of that pain and dependency of the oxygen tubes in the intensive care unit. One of my doctors said that I would die without the oxygen tube and that mean nurse who turned off the oxygen. Here in Heaven, I did not need help to breathe.

Now I was standing by the river that passes by the throne of God. I wanted to stay there forever and enjoy the sights. But somehow I knew that was not going to happen.

Heaven's Golden Vessel

Another piece of land was just as lovely and as beautiful as where I was standing. As I was looking at the other side of the river, I felt a gentle pull on my shoulders. I was being pulled back towards the golden vessel. As if to say, "Son, it is time for you to go back". It was as I was standing there enjoying that river, I looked across it, and there was pulling me very gently back, I was still looking at the other side of the river.

I started to wonder, "Where is my son Scott"? He was carjacked and killed in California. All of a sudden there was a pause and I looked on the other side of the river and to my amazement I saw my son Scott. He was standing there as if someone told him that his father was here and get over to the crystal river because he won't be here with us for long. There was my handsome son and I yelled to him, "Scott! It's you! You are alive".

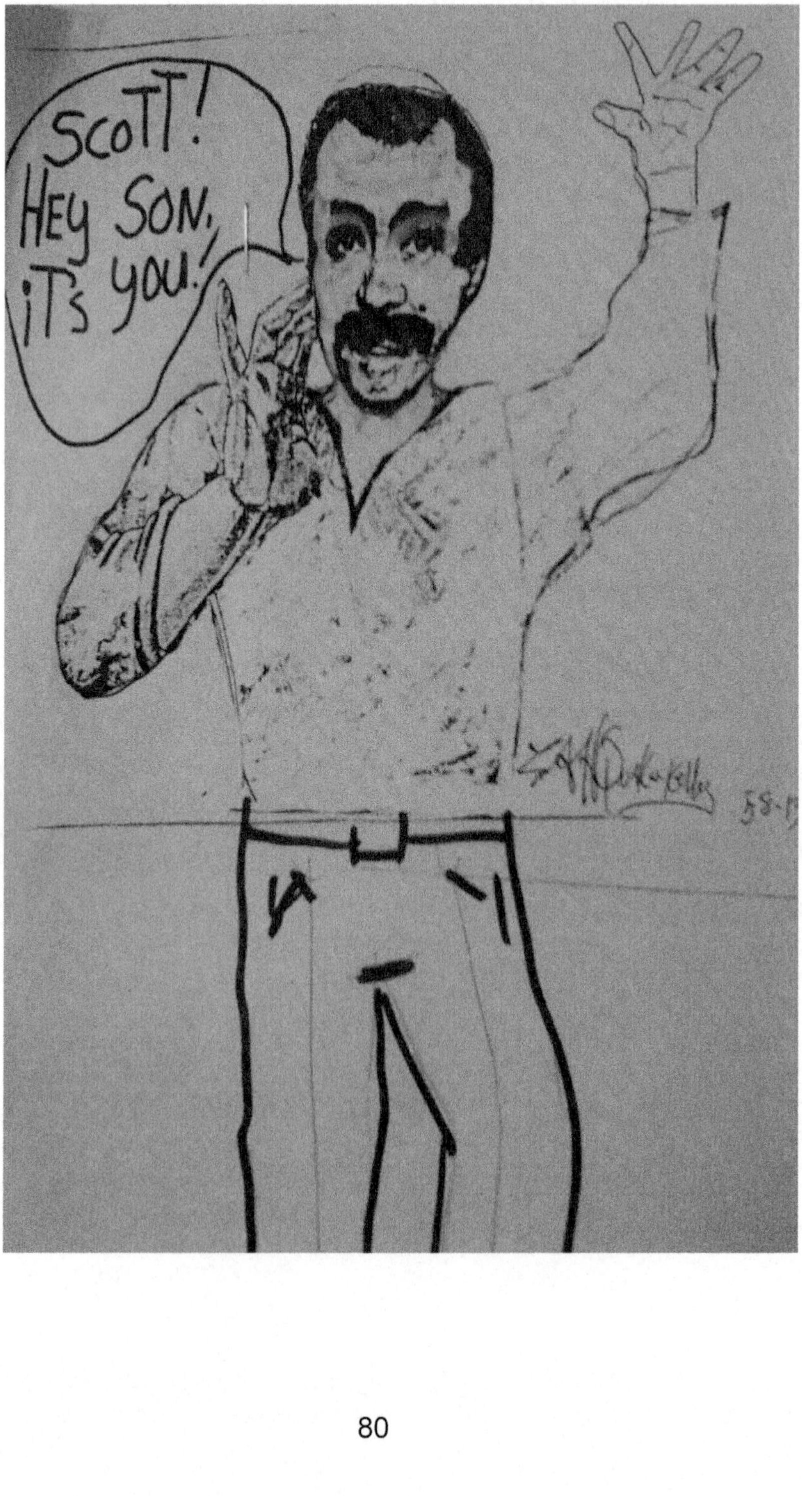
SCOTT!
HEY SON,
iT'S YOU!

He said, "Yes, Dad. Yes, I am alive". I said, "Son, this place is something". He said, "Dad, this is just like you and mom always told me it would be, but Dad, it is much more than words can tell". I was excited to see my son living and looking so good. I wanted to give him a big hug, like the one he gave me the day just before he was killed.

It was December 6, 1998. We were play boxing. He could never hit me. I was too fast for him. Then right in the middle of our play boxing and having so much fun, he got this sad distant look on his face. I said, "What's wrong, Son? What's wrong?" He grabbed me and gave me the biggest hug and said, "Dad, I love you." I said, "I love you too. Son, what's wrong? Did something happen on your job? Did somebody say something to hurt your feelings?" Scott said, "No Dad, nothing like that." I then said, "What is wrong then?" He said, "Dad, I am so proud of you and Mom." While he was hugging me so tight that I could hardly get any air in or out, he said, "Promise me something, Dad." I said, "Okay son, but what is wrong?" When each of my seven children hurt, I hurt.

Heaven's Golden Vessel

> DAD. REMEMBER BACK ON DECEMBER 6TH 1998. YOU GAVE ME YOUR WORD DAD. THAT YOU WOULD LET NOTHING STOP YOU FROM PREACHING DELIVERANCE. YOUR TIME IS NOT YET DAD. YOU MUST GO BACK AND FINISH THE WORK DAD. SO, MANY PEOPLE NEED YOUR HELP DAD.

EARTHQUAKE Kelley
3-4-16
I LOVE YOU 'SON.'

SURE miss you SON.

My son said, "Dad, I want you to promise me something. Promise me that you and Mom will never stop helping people. Dad, please do not ever stop preaching and teaching deliverance, no matter what people say or do to you. You and Mom are making such a big difference in the lives of so many people. Dad, promise me or I will never stop hugging you and let you go".

Heaven's Golden Vessel

The very next day my beloved son, Scott was killed. He loves Jesus and would do anything in the ministry. I miss him dearly. I wanted to get to him and hug him but there was that river of stained glass between us. I looked for something to sail over there but there was nothing. I said, "Son, where is the boat"? He said, "There is no boat coming for you Dad. You cannot come over here. You must go back Dad and finish the work that God has for you to do." I said, "No, son where is the boat"? He just repeated himself and added you promised me that you would not stop doing God's work and reminded me that I gave him my word.

Heaven's Golden Vessel

Chapter 11
The Testimony

Then there came a man that stood in front of my son. He was a man that went to be with the Lord in 2002. He was a father in the gospel to me. It was Elder Shumate. He said, "Son, you cannot come over to this side yet. Your time is not now. You must go back." In amazement, I asked, "Elder Shumate, is it you? My God, Elder Shumate." Then I saw other friends that were saved when they died. So many people came to the edge of the river. I got so excited to be there.
I saw a young black girl. She came to the edge of the river. I said to myself, "Who is this girl?" I don't know her. But about six months ago when I was in Birmingham, I was giving this testimony and I told the bishop there what happened to me. I don't know why I just so happened to be talking about all the wonderful things I saw in Heaven, but I told them about this young black girl that came to the bank of the river, but I did not know who she was.

They left the room and I thought that I said something to make them sad by bringing up a conversation that would remind them of someone that they missed that had died. They came back with a picture of a very beautiful young lady and showed it to me. I almost fell out of a chair. It was the girl that came to the edge of the river when my son and the other saints came to see me. I responded to them that girl in the picture is the same young lady at the river. It was the bishop's daughter, who went to be with Jesus a year ago. It is good to know that a family member is in Heaven with Jesus.

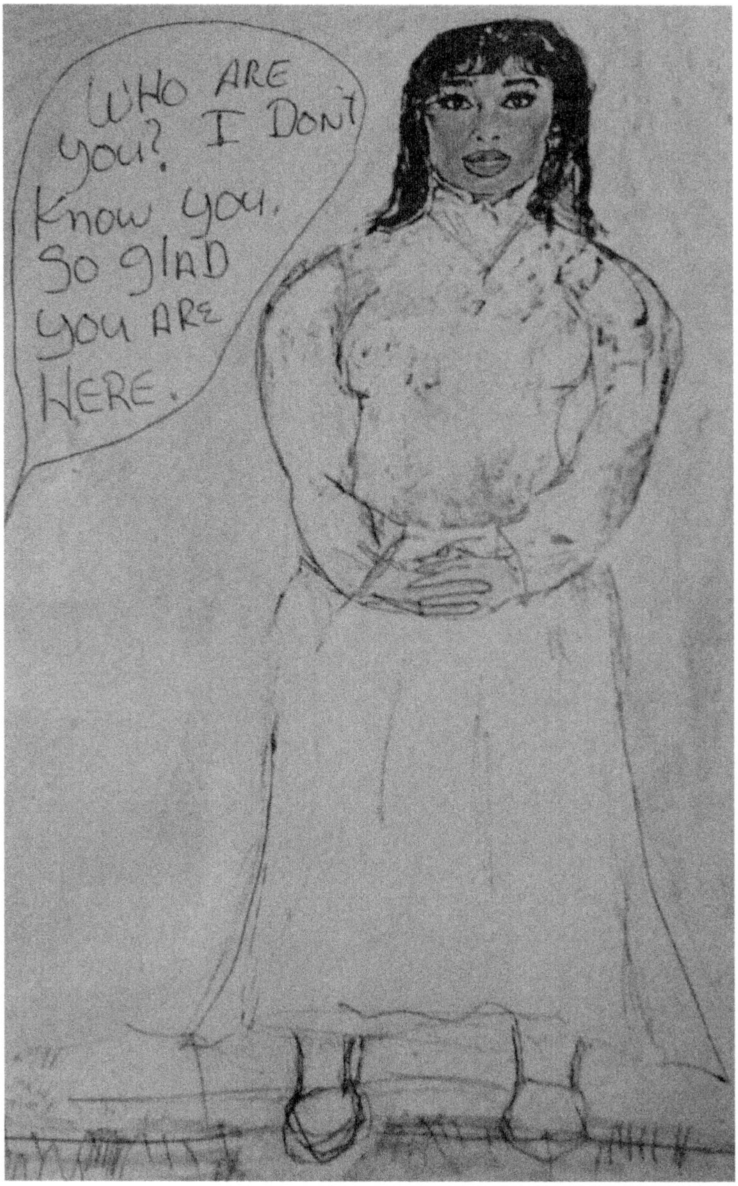
WHO ARE you? I DON'T Know you. So glAD you ARE HERE.

All of you that are reading this book, please don't ask me if I saw a family member of yours in Heaven. Sorry, that would be difficult to do, especially without the help of God.

I saw other people I knew that had died and gone to heaven and everyone was telling me to go back and finish God's work. I really did not want to hear that. On top of that, loving hands started pulling me back towards the golden vessel. I was trying to stay there with them.

Heaven's Golden Vessel

As I was still looking at the other side of the river, I saw children running and playing. I wanted to go play with them especially, because my ten year old nephew, Gary, was hit by a car in September 2004 and died. I knew without a doubt that Gary was playing with those children. If there was any playing to be done he would be there. I looked for him trying to spot him out among all of those millions of children running and playing. Somehow I knew my nephew was there. It had been more than nine months by now since Gary died. He would have played in all four Corners of paradise by now. You go Gary. I love you Gary.

UNCLE CURTIS, I'M HERE, DON'T WORRY ABOUT ME, I'M HERE I AM DOING FINE JESUS GOT ME.
I'M HAVING FUN!

Chapter 12
The Heart of God

Then there was another group of children that I saw running and jumping. I thought within myself, "Who are those children?" There appeared to be something a little different about those children. Then I heard a voice. It was clear to me that the voice was responding to my thoughts, and it said, "You are wondering who those children are." I was surprised at someone hearing my thoughts. I surprisingly responded by looking around and saying, "Yes, Lord." I knew it was God. I know His voice when I hear it. I asked, "Who are those children over there? They are a little different from the rest of the children in Heaven."

This was the first time God spoke to me in Heaven. He said, "These are the children that I sent down to Earth because of the hardness of man's heart, the sin of lust, hatred of me, and some of these children where aborted and sent back to me. Many in my church have had abortions in secret, they believe no one sees it but I see it all. Some of these children were murdered, sacrificed from witchcraft, died from disease, and many other things that happened to throughout the ages".

I could fell God's hurt and pain as He was telling me these things. I saw another side of God that I never knew existed. I had not realized that god could hurt like that over His creation. I felt sorry for Him in that moment. It hurt me to feel Him hurt.

That gentle hand that was pulling me away from the beautiful sights, people, and children finally reached the point to where I could no longer see anything. Somehow I knew I would return one day and stay forever.

Then God began to tell me, "You have a job to do on Earth. You must go back and tell the church of their sins and the things that they think are hidden, they are not hidden from me. Go back and tell the church of their wicked hidden lifestyles of lust, fornication, adultery, witchcraft in the church, rebellion, unforgiveness, lying, and hatred of one of another because of the color of their skin. Tell them to repent, pray and seek my face from the depths of their heart, and fast.

Heaven's Golden Vessel

As He spoke, I began to repent to God first for my lack of praying and fasting the way I used to. I started to cry out to God saying, Father, please forgive me I used to pray every day for over two hours".

In almost fifty years of living and almost thirty-five years of being saved, I have heard the sound of many things such as the sound of people in pain because I am a product of the street. As a child, I saw people being shot, killed, and one man had his face cut up right in front of me. I heard mothers scream as they heard that one of their loved ones passed. But in all my life, I never heard the sound of sorrow like I did when I heard the sound coming from the voice of God Himself over the condition of humankind and the sin coming up to Him from His church.

At first I asked God to send someone else to tell the church to repent but hearing God's voice was more than I can bear so I repented for not wanting to return to body back in the intensive care unit. I was overwhelmed with what God was saying, especially when He compared the church to someone having a broken leg and not going to the doctor for treatment.

He said, the more they walked on it, the worse it becomes. There is a spiritual dislocation of His people from Him because of the fractured relationship that sin has caused. Sin is and will continue to give the church trouble.

He reminded me of a scripture he gave me in the book of Romans, chapter six and verse one. Shall we continue in sin that grace may abound? God forbid". God said, "if this broken bone of sin is still not repented of, it will lead to discoloration or amputation". This means that you will be cut off from God.

He continued to say, sinners are dying every day and going to hell. He showed me a vision of a whole family in hell. I saw yellow and red flames covering their whole bodies. I heard them crying out in pain as they were biting their arms and pulling on each other trying to find relief. I felt so bad for that family because I know they will be spending eternity in hell.

Heaven's Golden Vessel

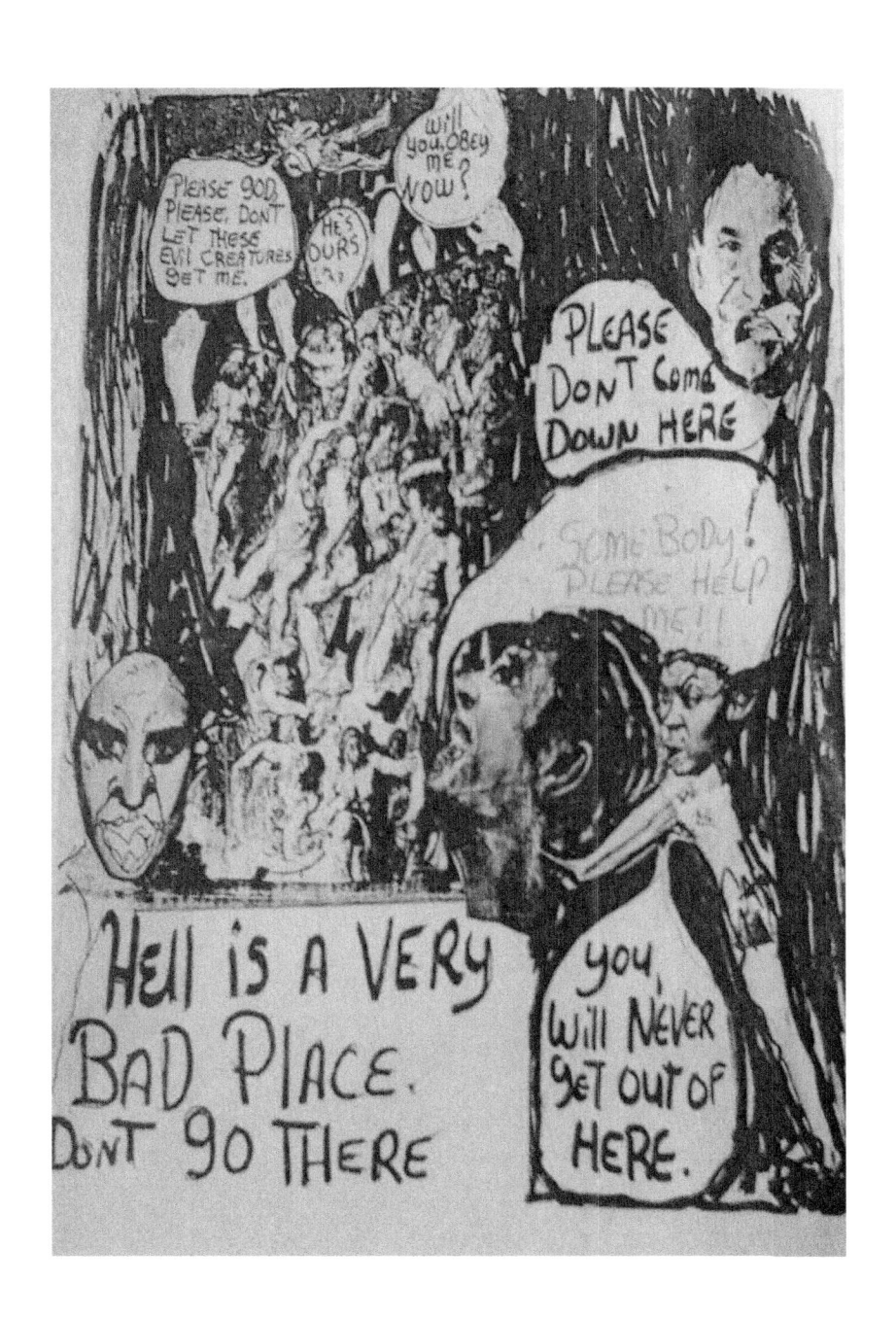

He told me to warn ministers that are only preaching for money and fame that they will be judged. He also said, "And tell them that I am removing my hand of mercy from them. I have given them many chances to repent, but many of them refused to repent. He told me that some have a wife and lovers on the side, some are homosexuals, and some practice the lifestyle of wife swapping in their minds and with their bodies. They say things like, "She can preach and sing better than my wife. How can I get rid of my wife and team up with her? I wish that my wife will die in a car crash, from a heart attack, or maybe she will die of breast cancer. I need 'Sister Blank" because we can do a powerful job for the Kingdom of Heaven. I sure hope my wife will die soon."

Heaven's Golden Vessel

Those who refuse to repent will die in their pulpits. Since January 2005 and the writing of this book, four preachers I know passed away in their pulpits. God said, "Unless those ministers in sin repent more will die. Death will come to them in different ways. Many of them are not taking me seriously by living any way they please". He said, "Tell them that unless they repent sickness and disease will not leave their bodies because one cursed by me, no prayer will help you".

I could feel the pain that God felt as He told me that many of His people are not seeking His face but they are seeking Him for what is in His hands. He said, "whole families will be lost in hell because they do not know me". I said, "God, who am I? They won't believe me." He would not argue with me. He said, "I am sending you back to warn them to repent and seek my face".

He continued to tell me to warn ministers that are only preaching for money and fame that they will be judged. I am removing my hand of mercy from them. I have given them many chances to repent, but many of them refused to repent. Some have a wife and lovers on the side, some are homosexuals, and some practice the lifestyle of swapping spouses in their minds and with their bodies. Say things like, "He or she can preach and sing better than my spouse, we can do a powerful job for the Kingdom of Heaven. How can I get rid of my husband or wife and team up with them? I wish that my husband or wife will die soon in a car crash, a heart attack, or maybe cancer.

There are people who have listened to My voice to repent on their death beds. Many people who died and are thought to have been lost in the eyes of some people are not in Hell. They repented before they drew their last breath and are now with me. Some of those people that you saw at the edge of the crystal river were some of those that heard my voice telling them to repent, they did and they are now with me in paradise.

Then there are some people who thought that they were saved when they died and are lost in the torments of Hell because they would not repent. He said, "They no longer see me as their Lord and Savior. They have turned from me."

Chapter 13

Chosen

God took my mind back about fifteen years ago, when my mother said, "Son, I have to tell you something. I waited until you were grown up to tell you this." I thought she was going to say I was adopted but know she told me a story of an evil doctor and another person that I will not mention. The two of them tried to get her to abort me but she refused. One of them kicked her in the stomach, dragged her down a flight of stairs, and threw her into a car. This person was much bigger and stronger than my mother.

Then she shared that there was another pair of hands working in her. They were the hands of the Lord protecting me from this abuse. They finally gave up because everything they tried had failed. God told me that it was His hands that hid me in my mother's womb. I am SO grateful and cannot thank Him enough. I will forever praise Him, I love Him So much.

He said, "I am sending you back to let them know that words have meaning. He brought back what happened to me so I could feel the pain on a personal level. He said, "Tell them that the world had been hiding behind words from the beginning by changing the words. For example, instead of saying sin, they use the word disease. Case in point, getting drunk is no longer a sin. It's a disease now. By removing the guilt for taking an unborn baby's life by changing the word baby to fetus, they make it look like a foreign thing, or just a mass of unwanted flesh.

Over the years, this word fetus found its way into our modern English language and into our schools where our children read it almost every day. The word has traveled from back alley abortion rooms to planned parenting clinics and then to the Supreme Court. Once they got a hold of this word, it became a part of our everyday word usage.

This word fetus is passed around dance halls, barber shops, at home, in our public schools, and in some church restrooms. It has also traveled between young girls who don't want to be mothers at age fifteen; and their mothers who don't want to be a young grandmother because they say it's just a fetus anyway not a real baby. Some men have bragged that their girlfriends have had more than ten abortions.

You can't go to Heaven like this. Some day we all will have to stand before God himself to be judged. If you know anyone that is guilty of these sins, tell them to repent before they die in their condition. He said, "Warn my church not to fall for this LIE that a baby is just a fetus".

God said, "Warn them." The Church and the world have bought into this deception. The kingdom of darkness has cheapened what used to be a prized event, having a baby. People used to delight in the fact that there was life growing inside of them. God is pulling covers off of every sinful thing that has been hidden, especially those living a hidden sinful lifestyle. I pray that you repent now before you are caught up in God's judgment.

Heaven's Golden Vessel

WHO ME BLOODY HANDS?
I. HAVE HAD OVER 10 ABORTION'S will GOD FORGIVE ME, FOR WHAT I HAVE DONE?
NO! NO. HE WONT
3-14-10

Heaven's Golden Vessel

The Word of God make it very clear what God is against and He will lift up your skirts over your face, showing the nations your nakedness and the kingdoms your shame. (Nahum 3:4-6) This kind of nakedness means that you are not clothed with righteousness.

The Word of God also says that He will cast abominable filth upon you, make you vile and spectacle. (Nahum 3:6+7) Abominable filth is not only trash but it is life filled with dirt. There will always be some type of drama connected with you or just the mention of your name brings disgusting thoughts to the ears and mind of the hearer. If you do not turn toward God, you will always find yourself at the fork in the road until you give your heart over to God.

I could still hear the hurt in the voice of the Lord as I thought to myself, "I see why the Lord destroyed humankind before. It hurts God to His heart that there are people who will go after sex with such lust that they will pull anything out at the roots that stands in their way. They go from one relationship to another like it is some kind of ship on a voyage. They must conquer every bed that they can lie upon with not a care of what God thinks.

I said, "Oh God, I did not know that the world hurt you so". Then God said, "Warn my Church and those who have deviated from my Word about changing their attitude of seeking after me to just being accepted in unholy social crowds; where there are no morals and no standards. God said that many have departed from the straightway and the course that He has called them to take. Many people treat my Word trivially and believe it is no big deal. But do not know that is what the kingdom of darkness wants because it is after your soul". The enemy of our souls starts with our bodies then he works on our minds. This is one of the traps from the pits of hell to get us from the Word of God so that we would end up in abusive and other evil things, including suicide". God wants us to repent so He would clean away all the shame and remove the guilt.

He showed me that many people in the Church don't want to show any untimely blemishes on their bodies. They will do anything to stay young. Some are close to selling their souls to Satan right in the Church. No Father! Not in the Church! He says, "Yes, because they want money and they are not willing to wait on me." God told me that no amount of money can remove the thorn that is stuck in your mind. He said that sin has caused my people to be imprisoned inside of themselves.

They have become their own idols, and the spirit behind this worship of self is of the kingdom of darkness. God told me that Satan is directly behind it all. I felt so bad for our Creator, then I thought, "Lord, why would you create something that would hurt you so much"? Then I remembered that God gives us free will.

Suppose you raised a child and gave him the best of everything. Then at the age of fifteen, he pulls out a shot gun and wounds his mother because she did not give him what he wanted. Would this not hurt you? The Lord said, "some have cursed me in their hearts because I did not answer them as fast as they wanted me to answer".

He brought to my mind the scripture that I had read many times, Malachi 3:13, it says, "Your words have been stout against me." I looked up the word stout and it means stubborn, hurtful, determined to be bold against, and very dark, evil and mean words. He told me that there are people holding things against Him like He is a human being. The Lord said, "They think I have promised them something then lied to them." He said, "I never lie." He also said, "Some were yelling to me while on their knees saying you let my mother die. You let me down! Why did you let momma leave me?"

He said, "Some are on their knees cursing His name and vowing to never pray to me again; cursing me in their hearts because all of their pregnancies ended in miscarriages; blaming me for losing their jobs; yelling up to Him that He don't care, He must want me to be poor; some give him a day and a time to come through or they will do something evil to get money; many blame Him for not being married; some are blaming Him for being alone; and some are blaming Him for being molested or raped". Many have asked me, "where were you when I needed you, I hate you, including people in the church"?

He told me that many people in the church have hate in their heart toward me. Every day, some preachers say, "why is it taking so long for my ministry to launch out, where is my car, where is my house, why do I have cancer, and why haven't you healed me yet?

The Lord said, "people say such mean and evil things about and to me. You must go back and tell them that they cannot receive from me as long as they are holding things against me. They cannot receive from me and hate me in their hearts. They must repent." God said, "I am a perfect holy God and upright who has never sinned. The ministers who are holding things against me must realize that their ministries will never soar until they forgive me even though I never sinned against them or against anyone."

I said, "Please Lord, send somebody else. Who am I to tell them Lord? You have so many great preachers living on Earth. Lord I am here with you; I want to stay. Plus they won't listen to me. Lord, I have tried to preach deliverance for years, and many have all but shot at me in many churches."

Chapter 14
The Reminder

Then he showed me a vision of people burning in Hell's fire. He let me hear the screaming, and I saw the flames. The fire was so hot I could feel the heat. I saw the looks on the faces of those there. Many of them were from churches who only preached things to satisfy the flesh.

God said, "Son, remember back in 1971 when you died of an overdose of drugs and those evil spirits that pulled your soul out of your body and down to hell, where you lifted up your eyes? (Luke 16:22-24) Do you remember the pain and the torment, son"? I said, "Yes Lord, I will never forget. You came down to hell to get me and as you were pulling me out those demons long fingernails were trying to stay in me to keep me in hell. You spared my soul from hell so that I could be used to win souls from a fate was surely mine.

Heaven's Golden Vessel

God asked me a question that hit me like a boxing glove, "Can you turn your back on those that will be lost forever unless you go, preach, and minister to them and warn them of what will take place soon"?

He said, "Many good unsaved church folks will be there because they went to church, but they never accepted me in their hearts". There are many good people, but just doing good deeds will not get you into Heaven. You must be saved, born again."

He said, "There are many evil fathers who are controlling their families by letting them go just to mock it. Many fathers are leading their families to Hell.

I said, "Father, forgive me for not wanting to go back because many of those church folks hurt me so much. God, they almost had me to a place that I did not care what happened to them even if they went to Hell, because I was so hurt so much by the church. Father, there are some mean people in the church. I don't want to be hurt anymore. Father God, if this means so much to you for me to go back and tell them what you said then Lord God, I will go and continue to preach and teach deliverance".

Chapter 15

When I Got Back

As I turned to my right, I found myself standing next to the beautiful golden vessel. The door opened for me and the angels were smiling at me as I sat down. Then the door gently closed and within a blink of an eye, I was back laying in the hospital, in the intensive care unit. I still had the headache but I was glad that God saw something in me to place such a huge charge in my lap.

As I was looking up to heaven, praising God, I heard God say to me, "you must take this mandate seriously"! He instructed me to keep my heart clean no matter what people say or do and just forgive them. If you can forgive the man that killed your son than you can forgive those that hurt you in the churches too." I gave God my word in that hospital that I would tell the world what He told me. God told me that He would hold me to my word so I made up in my mind to share my experience everywhere I go.

When my wife came to pick me up, I walked by the nurses' station. They were sharing how they did not think that I was ever going home. One doctor believed I would die within twenty-four hours. Another doctor said, "No, let him go home. If something happens to him, he can always be brought back to the hospital. But I said, "No doctor, I will only come back to visit or to pray for others."

As my wife was driving me home, it looked like I had arrived in a strange city for the first time. I could hardly recognize the streets that I know I have driven down so many times. My vision was affected by this experience and it hurt to keep my eyes open so I would just keep them closed most of the time. My children were so good to me. The doctors continued to call and check on me weeks after this experience, we became like a family.

The doctors told my wife to make sure I take a particular pill every day. They were hard to find because every drug store did not carry them. They were used to shrink the blood vessels that had burst in my head because if it did not shrink I would bleed to death. Then I thought about the blood of Jesus that He shed for us all. I know it was hard for him to let his blood flow, but if he didn't we would not have the hope of our healing from every sickness or disease.

Lord, thank you for dying for me. I hung on to what I knew in God's Word in spite of what the doctors were telling us about only having six weeks to live. When I lived beyond the six weeks, they were waiting to only give me another death sentence. Each time I lived beyond the sentence, they gave me another. It was like a game, and I called it the "Outlive What the Doctor Says" game.

Then it was time for my first private doctor's visit. The doctor had me sit on the examining table. She said, "Do you know that you are in very bad shape? Most people do not live past two weeks, do not fool yourself you are very sick. You had a hemorrhage of the brain and it is the worst kind known to man. You must be on a diet that will not make you constipated or you will die in the bathroom. People with your kind of sickness, no one survive". She got mad at me and put her hand on my forehead and told me to stop frowning in my forehead because it will send the blood flow up to my brain and I will die. She ended her examination and said, "you only have to Mr. Kelley, you are very sick"!

MR. Kelley YOU ARE SICK! Very Sick! STOP Frowning up your
You Will Die if
THis LADY is NUTS
5-17-13

When we got home, my wife said, "Baby, do not pay any attention to what she says, she is not God. God sent you back here to do a work for Him and that is all there is to it. How could she say that you have a short time to live! God said my husband shall live and not die. He sent you back and said you will have a very long life. So where did she get her information from?"

Today, I am sitting here in my home and writing this book, "Heaven's Golden Vessel". I am almost back to my fighting state. Where is that big George Foreman? No George, my professional fighting days are over. The only fighting I will do now will be against sin. I will now fight to help the hungry, witness to gang members about the love of Jesus, visit the hospitals and the prisons, and impact the streets of Hollywood.

I have preached from New York City to Los Angeles. People have been repenting. Pastors and their congregations have been repenting and crying out to God to forgive them of their sin. I am just getting started and anticipate what God is going to do through me next.

Prayer of Confession

Lord, I repent of my sins. I believe in my heart that Jesus is God's son and he died for me as the final sacrificial lamb, and I believe God raised him from death, and he now sits on the right hand of the Father. His blood covers my past, present, and future sins. Father, thank you for loving me so much. Amen.

Now find a local community of believers to share your confession of belief and to help you with your daily walk.

Name: _____

Date of Confession: _____

ABOUT AUTHOR

Dr. Curtis "Earthquake" Kelley is one of eleven children born in Stamford, Connecticut to Robert and Erma Jean Kelley. Earthquake's Haitian father was a practitioner of Voodoo, Obeya, and Hoodoo. He was forced to learn over one hundred witchcraft concepts. His mother was a praying woman who would anoint him with olive oil in the middle of the night. His father beat her many times for defending her son with prayer from witchcraft. Earthquake thanks God for a praying mother.

He started using drugs at the age of four, he started smoking marijuana at the age of six, and because two of his brothers were dealers, they introduced him to cocaine at the age of ten. These early experiences led to a life of dealing and using drugs. After overdosing on drugs, Earthquake gave his life to the Lord at a revival meeting in Milwaukee, Wisconsin on December 15, 1971.

At the age of fourteen, Earthquake walked into a gym in downtown Stamford. A great boxer approached him saying, "I know who you are, if you get serious with fighting, you will become a great boxer and go far with it" and he did become a boxer.

Earthquake founded a substance abuse ministry called, "The B.R.I.D.G.E." in Carson, California. It had moved to the West Adams Foursquare Church, under the pastoral leadership of the late H. Marvin and Juanita Smith. In 1991, Earthquake founded, "The Bridge of Hope Church. In 2005, the ministry became known as "Bridge of Deliverance".

Heaven's Golden Vessel– By Dr. Curtis "Earthquake" Kelley

Available on amazon.com and e-store createspace.com

Dr. Curtis "Earthquake" Kelley

is available for conferences, seminars, and workshops

Dr. Curtis "Earthquake" Kelley also works side by side in ministry with his wife Selena Kelley and they are available for Revivals, Conferences, Seminars, Youth Women and Men's Retreats

Contact information:

Dr. Curtis "Earthquake" Kelley

P.O. Box 1192 Littlerock, California 93543

www.earthquakekelleyministries.com

books I recommend

(available on Amazon) & (e-store www.createspace.com)

Escaping the N'Mos Cycle by Dr. Curtis "Earthquake" Kelley

The Dangers of Profanity by Dr. Curtis "Earthquake" Kelley

*****

Overcoming the Tamar Syndrome by Selena Kelley (Coming Soon)

*****

Cycles of Victory by Chandler Kelley Miller

Spiritual Healing for Women and Men by Chandler Kelley Miller

The Night the Angels Danced by Chandler Kelley Miller

Domestic Violence Spiritual Healing by Chandler Kelley Miller

*****

Why Submit to a Lie
by Evangelist Andra Walker

*****

Coming Away From Beggarly Elements by Prophet Ascari Walker

Printed in Great Britain
by Amazon